HONOLULU, APRIL 27TH, 1877.

To His Excellency

The Minister of the Interior.

SIR:

The undersigned, Commissioners appointed by His Majesty the King in Privy Council under the Act "To aid in the development of the resources of the Kingdom," approved on the 25th day of September, A. D. 1876, would respectfully report.

The Commissioners, in pursuance of the first Section of said Act, left Honolulu on the 20th day of February, 1877, on Her Britannic Majesty's Ship "Fantome," which vessel had been kindly tendered by H. B. M.'s Commissioner and Consul General, Major James H. Wodehouse, to convey the Commission to Hawaii.

DISTRICT OF KOHALA.

The Commission landed at Mahukona on February 20th, and on the following day proceeded to Kohalaloko. The agricultural resources of Kohala are well known through the success which has attended the enterprises there established, which were visited by the Commission. The Union Sugar Mill of Mr. Hinds, conducted on the principle of grinding on shares the cane grown by others, has proved profitable to both planters and mill owner, and is a valuable illustration of the success of this principle.

Mr. Hinds is about erecting another mill to be conducted the same way, and the operations of the present mill will probably be enlarged.

These opportunities have stimulated the people in the neighborhood to increased industry, and the prospect of large returns for the capital and labor invested will doubtless lead to bringing into cultivation a larger area of cultivated land.

The Kohala Sugar Company, a corporation cultivating entirely on their own account, are prosecuting the planting of cane and the manufacture of sugar with great energy. The lands in this immediate neighborhood are mostly taken up, and the cultivation of sugar is being extended to parts formerly considered unfavorable for cultivation, but where experience shows good results; and we think there is still opportunity for profitable investment. Dr. Wight is vigorously enlarging and improving the capacity of his fine estate.

C. F. Hart, Esquire, the local Circuit Judge, is pushing forward a co-operative enterprise on the lands of Makapala and Niulii, which are mostly cultivated by native Hawaiians for their own account, to be ground on shares at a mill to be erected by Judge Hart. The land is very rich, and is said never to have suffered from drought. There is little doubt of large crops of sugar-cane. Its vales are filled with tropical growth and it bears large crops of taro. It is greatly to be hoped that this enterprise will meet with such success as will stimulate others of a like nature, for the good of the people as well as the development of the country. Between Niulii and the valley of Pololu, the farthest land in this direction visited by the Commission, the lands are fertile and are far from being fully developed.

The Commission were struck with the hopefulness displayed by the people of this district, a marked contrast to the listlessness and apathy observed in districts where no agricultural enterprises are prosecuted, and illustrating the important influence which the encouragement of such enterprise and industry will have on the preservation of the Hawaiian race, who in some districts have little to hope for or live for.

The quantity of land in this district capable of cultivation is very hard to estimate, as experience constantly demonstrates new capacities. Cane is successfully cultivated now at higher altitudes than was for a long while deemed expedient and in parts of the district formerly considered too dry. Upland taro grows high upon the slopes of Makapala and Niulii, and thousands of acres yet uncultivated are doubtless capable of producing taro, sugar, coffee and other products. The climate is healthy, cool and inviting. The supply of water in the northerly part of the district is limited, and some steps will yet be necessary for the preservation of the forests in the mountains.

Mr. Hinds we are told was successful in finding a supply of water for his new mill by digging in a gulch near by. This shows the value of intelligent effort to seek subterranean supplies, which should encourage like effort in other places.

The Commission recommend that the bridges connecting the

lands of Makapala and Niulii be replaced by wider and stronger ones, and that the roads in that neighborhood be graded with the view of facilitating the cartage of cane; also that the Government assist in laying a buoy and mooring at Dr. Wight's landing, in consideration of its being kept open and the roads leading thereto for the public use.

The Commission carefully examined the landing at Honoipu. The boat landing is on the side of a point of lava rock which makes out for some 300 feet or more from the shore, over which the surf breaks at times with great force, so as to render any structure of reasonable cost impracticable. The anchorage is good, and vessels can lay safely,—even at times when with present facilities a boat could not safely lay to land cargo. The Commission recommend that a boat dock be blasted out of the lava rock, say 40 feet long by 15 feet wide, with a depth of five feet at lowest water—where the present landing stage is. Examination shows that a cave exists under the rock, which lessens by a great deal the amount of rock to be removed. It is believed that such a dock would often enable the shipping and landing of merchandise on occasions when with present facilities the landing would be useless, and thus promote the welfare of the district. The cost of such a dock is estimated from such data as was obtained at $1500. The Commission also recommend that the landing at Mahukona be improved by blasting out the rocks which obstruct the boat channel.

The roads of this district show intelligent care, and reflect credit upon Mr. Holmes, the road supervisor.

The introduction of a few hundred families of a laboring class to enable the enterprising people, native and foreign of Kohala, to prosecute with vigor their plans, would tend more than anything else to develop the resources of this district.

WAIMEA.

From Puuhue the Commission proceeded to Waimea. The route lies around the slopes of the Kohala mountains through Kawaihae-uka. The forests on the Kohala mountains are dying rapidly. The land is used mostly for grazing purposes, though on the mountain potatoes of fine quality can be raised in large quantities. In sheltered places, coffee would doubtless grow,—but owing to the sparseness of the population and the superior attractions of other parts of the district, this part will hardly soon be settled. The once fertile and populous plain of Waimea looked sterile and desolate when visited by the

Commission,—a painful contrast to Kohalaloko on the other side of the mountain.

The grazing interest, so paramount here, is fatal to agricultural enterprise. The diminution of the water supply and other results caused by the wasting of the forests, have led the people to seek other homes. At a meeting of the people held on the 26th February, at the Court House at Waimea, there was great complaint made before the Commission regarding the supply and quality of the water used by the people, and a desire expressed that the Commission recommend the Government to take steps to remedy the evils complained of. Although not perhaps strictly within the range of their duties under the Act to develop the resources of the Kingdom, the Commissioners, regarding the importance of this matter upon the health and prosperity of the district and the future possible development of its resources, visited the stream and followed it to the point where it is divided.

The complaint of the people is well founded. The water they use is fouled in many places by cattle, horses and other animals, and as the stream is sluggish it has no chance to free itself of impurities, and the water used by the people in their houses must be a cause of disease and death, especially to the children. It is true that it is possible for the people by going a long distance to get purer water, but it is well known that but few will take that trouble, nor does it seem right that they should be compelled to. It is little wonder that, with his crops trodden out by the sheep or cattle of his stronger neighbours, his family sickened perhaps to death by the polluted waters, that the small holder should yield to despair, and abandoning his homestead seek employment in some other district, usually without making another home.

The Commission would report that in their opinion, for the good of the district the water should be taken by Government and made available to the people through pipes or covered conduits, secure from animal intrusion. The animals should be watered from the conduits in troughs. Mills, tanneries and other mechanical enterprises should be supplied by pipes.

The plains of Pukapu and Waimea are subject to high winds, aggravated by the loss of the sheltering forests of former days. The soil however is very good in many places for sugar cane and other products. To develop its best resources, efforts must be made to restore the forests and husband the supply of water at their sources to furnish a supply for agricultural purposes. At present the lands are used almost exclusively for grazing purposes. Although the proprietors and lessors are probably not averse to the establishment of agricultural enterprises, it is to be feared that the denudation of the neighboring mountains and plains of the forests will render the climatic conditions unfavorable to success.

It would seem that a wise appreciation of the best interests of this district, even of the grazing interests themselves, would lead to the decrease of the immense herds which threaten not only Waimea but even Hamakua with almost irreparable disaster. It is to be feared that they will in time render a large part of the land of little value even for grazing purposes, owing to the increasing frequency and severity of droughts and consequent failure of springs. Some thousands of cattle are said to have died this last winter from want of water, and the works erected in Waimea for the purpose of trying out cattle have been idle for months for want of water.

The Commission do not propose here to discuss fully the vexed questions of the causes of the diminution of the forests, but in view of the fact that they are diminishing and that the streams and springs diminish in a corresponding ratio, also that with the cattle running upon the lands as at present, any effort to restore them must be futile and any hopes of their recuperation vain, the Government, if it would wish to preserve that part of the island of Hawaii from serious injury, must take some steps for reclaiming the forests.

In this connection we would say, that it is unfortunate that large tracts of Crown and Government lands have been lately leased on long terms for grazing purposes, without conditions as to their protection from permanent injury, at rates much below their value even as preserves for Government purposes or public protection.

The Commission deem this a matter of grave importance, challenging the earnest attention of the Government, and involving the prosperity of two important and valuable districts.

There are large quantities of fallen trees in the forests, whose removal would doubtless be of benefit to the forests and it would seem could be profitably taken to Honolulu for sale as firewood.

HAMAKUA.

On the 27th of February, the Commission visited Waipio Valley and rode through it. This valley is rich in waters which are fed from springs in the valley itself. The falls of Hiilawe were dry, which is a remarkable circumstance. The capacity of the valley for the production of taro to supply the Districts of Hamakua, Waimea, and even Kohala, is large, and it would seem to offer every advantage to its people. A few acres of land are adapted to cane and coffee. The palis on either side are steep, and it would be well to furnish some aid to the people by buoys, so that a surf boat could be used in getting their produce out of the valley for shipment. This would seem the better way, as although a fair road for pack animals might be made up the pali, it would be expensive, and there would be a long distance to traverse to a port of shipment. About a mile to the southeast of Waipio is a landing sometimes used, called Honokaape, but as its use would not be more convenient or safe than a surf boat at Waipio, the Commission did not think it well to advise the construction of a road to it. The landing at Honomalino was examined, but no improvement suggested, as anything which would be available in weather when the landing can not now be used, would be of very great cost. The land of Waikoekoe, held by S. Parker, seems admirably adapted for a large sugar plantation, and the usual products of high lands,—soil rich and laying well. The lands between Waipio and Waikoekoe have patches of good land for sugar and other products.

The landing of Kaihumoku was examined, but not considered, under present circumstances, a place to expend any money upon, though if a plantation was started in the neighborhood it would doubtless be used in good weather for light freight. The land of Kapulena is rough and stony on the lower part, though above the road it has several hundred acres of fair land for cane or coffee. The landing at Honokaai has the best natural advantages for the construction of a break-water, having some large rocks laying just awash in a position to be utilized. The boat harbor, which could be thus sheltered, would need to be cleared by blasting some large rocks, and as material for a break-water would have to be brought from some distance the expense would be very great, and the landing at Honokaa would be near enough for the use of the land of Honokaai, which seems to be adapted for cane, though hilly. Its sheltered ravines will grow coffee, oranges and other tropical fruit. Kawele was recommended as a landing, but is simply a point of rocks running into the sea, giving but little shelter in any wind. Honokaa is the site of the plantation of Messrs. Siemsen & Marsden, on which there is good cane growing, showing what under proper cultivation the district may produce. The scarcity of water for mechanical purposes is a great drawback to the district, which being blessed with frequent showers, does not suffer from drought, but is singularly deficient in springs and running streams. This want can be remedied by reservoirs, or by wells in the gulches like that sunk by Mr. Hinds in Kohala. This is merely a matter of enterprise and industry. Parties should provide themselves with reservoirs, but the Commission would recommend that a careful survey be made for water supply for the district at Government expense; that the supplies, if found, may be controlled by Government and used in the way best adapted to aid in developing the district. Just back of Honokaa Plantation is a large tract of 10,000 or more acres of Government land in forest, which is unfortunately leased for grazing purposes, and unless the lease is cancelled in some way great damage must result to the district. The landing at Honokaa is the best, so far seen in the district. The Commission would recommend that the landing be improved by erecting a sloping sea wall of concrete to protect the road to the present derrick, which should be replaced by a substantial iron derrick capable of raising eight tons weight, and a road of easy grade laid out to the Government road, which, under a competent road maker, can be so laid out as to furnish access to most of the lands of the district. At this point heavy machinery can be landed, except at exceptional times, and carted to any part of the district, while light freight can be landed at the landings heretofore mentioned when the weather is favorable, or by a rope buoyed off from the shore. Mahiki and Paauhau were examined as landings. The former would require a large outlay for a road to it. Paauhau is doubtless one of the finest lands in the district, presenting many advantages for one or two sugar plantations. Beyond this land is some stony land intermixed with very good land till Kaholalele is reached. Some 10,000 acres of forest land belonging to Government lie between Kalopa and Kaohe, which are not yet leased. It is to be hoped this will be reserved and protected from trespass. Kohala-lele has some fine cane land, and the landing offers another opportunity for the erection of a derrick, which will be necessary, as several large gulches intervene between this part of the district and that which would be secured by the landing at Honokaa. There should be a platform of concrete laid on the rocks some fifteen or twenty feet above the sea for the derrick, and a track from the platform some five hundred feet to the top of the dug-way, on an incline, with a hoisting winch and cable.

The District of Hamakua may become a most productive district. In commenting on lands we have spoken of them as sugar lands, as that will doubtless be the staple product; but there is almost no land that is not cultivatable, and everywhere the fruits of the tropics and many of the temperate zone can be raised. The land is rolling, not so level as generally represented, and the Government road is an illustration of the folly of appointing incompetent road-makers and supervisors. There are no insuperable obstacles to the construction of a good cart road from Waipio to Paauhau, and it should be built. All the roads in the district show shameful neglect. The fact that most all the finest lands back of the district are held by graziers, whose immense herds are already making inroads upon them, is full of danger to the prosperity of Hamakua, which should at any cost be saved from the fate of Waimea. The law under which the Commission acts, provides that cultivated lands should be taxed for improvements, but in a district like this it would be manifestly unjust that the small amount of cultivated land should pay taxes while the great bulk of the lands more valuable should escape because their proprietors fail to develop them; and your Commissioners would suggest that lands capable of cultivation should bear their taxation according to their value, as otherwise an unfair discrimination is made against industry and enterprise. Here, as elsewhere, the great requisite is population,—people to develop the resources of the district which ought to sustain a population of 10,000 in easy circumstances. Where mills are established on the factory principle of grinding for cultivators of small tracts, every encouragement should be given and aid extended in the way of the improvements suggested. As to the amount of land capable of cultivation, there are doubtless many thousands of acres, but in the absence of accurate surveys no estimate can be made. There is doubtless sufficient cane land to raise sugar cane enough for ten to fifteen mills.

DISTRICT OF HILO.

The first point examined in this district was the proposed landing at Ookala. A gulch runs down to the shore, where it ends in a cliff some 200 feet high. To the eastward of the gulch a small point of land makes out into the sea with a projecting reef of rocks, making a small cave which is smooth in ordinary weather and affording an opportunity for a derrick. The cliff is very precipitous and overhangs the sea in places. A road of tolerable grade can be constructed from the landing along the side of the cliff to the foot of the gulch, and roads from that point up to both sides of the gulch to reach the adjoining lands of Kaiwiki and Kaala on one side, Ookala, Humuula and Waipimalei on the other. These lands are taken up already for cane planting.

At Laupahoehoe the landing is very good and the lands rich. Messrs. Lidgate and Campbell have fine cane growing and every prospect of success in their enterprise at this place. The roads on the

Laupahoehoe palis should be improved. From this, to the land of Maulua on the lands of Koamano, Lauhulu, Kihalani and Papaaloa, Hookumahoe and others are very fine lands. Some of the lands are let and some 1000 acres sold, but there are some 3000 acres cane land left in the vicinity, of Government lands, making some 4000 acres in all; also from 10,000 to 15,000 acres of forest lands, which should be preserved. If parties could be induced to put up a mill on the central factory system on one of these lands, and the rest let out to small farmers, an admirable opportunity would be given to parties of small means and to the native Hawaiians in the vicinity. Probably Hawaiians in other parts of the district would gather here if such a prospect was held out, and the same happy results which have occurred in Kohala ensue. The Government lands, or such parts as were reserved, would become of greater value and yield a good rental. An enterprise of this kind in each district would be invaluable in establishing centres of influence and society, which would attract emigration, demonstrate the capacity of the soil, and thus give a value to all the surrounding lands. There is no lack of water, and with good roads to Laupahoehoe there would be no trouble about shipping produce. On the forest land back of these lands there is a large extent of coffee lands. The Commission would recommend that the Government lands here be devoted to the effort to establish a central factory, and to promote immigration; also that part of it be reserved till Legislative authority can be obtained to allot it in small parcels to immigrants. At Kaiakea there is a good landing, which would require a road to connect and a mooring buoy. Next to the land of Maulua there are some 1000 acres of good cane land belonging to Government. All these lands should be surveyed and devoted to the development of this rich district. The Commission earnestly recommend that the Government Surveyors be instructed to survey the coast line and the Government road, which would give correct initial points for other surveyors to work from in prosecuting surveys. Surveyors should be sent for from abroad to prosecute this work if necessary. Some of them would probably settle on some of the lands, and be valuable additions to the population of the district. The Government should have on roads, landings and surveys, a dozen or more civil engineers as soon as practicable. The landing at Hakalau was examined. An iron pier to connect the beach with a point of lava on the east side of the bay, would give a fair landing, but the expense would be great; as well as connecting roads up the palis. If mills were put in the gulch it would be advisable to make the landing available for surf boats. The Government have about

1500 acres of good land in the vicinity, and there is a larger quantity of lands belonging to private parties.

At Honomu, in ordinary weather, a good landing can be made in a surf boat, and would only need a buoy; parties are projecting a small plantation on this land with a mill in the gulch. There are some 1500 acres of Government land in the vicinity, and some 1250 sold to private parties, some of which is cane land. The establishment of a good mill at Honomu would greatly add to the value of these lands. From this land on to Hilo the land is largely under cultivation, the plantations of Kaupakuea, Onomea, Papaekou and Paukaa lying along here. On these estates the introduction of new canes and methods of cultivation have shown the capacity of the lands to produce large crops, and their prospects are very flattering. They will doubtless become very valuable estates, and show what with labor can be accomplished in this district, many of the best lands of which are yet undeveloped. Back of these plantations lie large lands adapted to coffee culture. The coffee plantation of Mr. William Kinney is an evidence of the great value of this land for this product, and demonstrates what can be accomplished by energy, even without a large capital. Mr. Kinney has now growing on eighty acres some 100,000 coffee trees in splendid condition, and in the neighborhood of his plantation,—in fact the whole belt of land lying in the back part of the Hilo District, ranging from 1000 to 2000 feet above the level of the sea, is capable of equal cultivation. In our opinion, this land for the purpose of coffee cultivation is equal to any in the world. The abundant supply of water gives valuable facilities for fluming the berries to the beach, where the necessary machinery and appliances for cleaning and drying could be erected. If such flumes were erected and appliances furnished to clean and prepare the coffee at fair rates or on shares, and the lands then thrown open to actual cultivators, a great opportunity would be offered to settlers, and the value of the lands greatly enhanced to their proprietors.

The Commission would recommend that Government lands in that district be surveyed and let to actual cultivators in alternate sections, with such conditions as may be necessary to reserve water and rights of way for flumes, and the balance reserved to offer in smaller lots to immigrants after the sections first disposed of are under cultivation, and the value of the business demonstrated.

The lands will produce abundantly of kalo with little labor, which is a profitable crop, and settlers with small means can raise most of their requirements, while the coffee trees are maturing, which they will do in three years; after four years the crop would be continuous and yield a regular income.

The Commission would recommend a pier north of the present steamer wharf at Waiakea, in Hilo Bay, built in a substantial manner, extending some 200 feet from a rocky point there, so that vessels could lay alongside. The produce of the district could be brought to Hilo for shipment to foreign markets, thus making a great saving to the people of the district. Hilo should be the shipping port of this large and rich district, and a wise expenditure here would increase the value of property and tend to make the district what it should be, second in wealth and importance to none other in the Kingdom.

The Commission believe that many of the improvements recommended for the Hamakua and Hilo Districts, should be begun as soon as possible, to give confidence in the intention of the Government to carry them on and give an impetus to enterprise, especially with regard to mills to grind on shares cane raised by small cultivators. Natives show a commendable zeal to cultivate on their own account, which should be encouraged wherever possible. Immediate steps should also be taken for the introduction of laborers, that enterprises may be undertaken, and especially to bring into the Kingdom a class of people who would bring their families and perhaps assimilate with the Hawaiian race. Probably in India such could be found, and the Commission would earnestly recommend that Government lands be reserved to give such, if after completing their contracts of service they would settle on them and cultivate them. As in the case of Hamakua District, good lands are spoken of as cane lands or coffee lands; but these lands are adapted to the cultivation, in many places, of oranges, limes and other fruits. Forests of Sumach are growing wild, and as this has been said to be the Sumach of commerce, which when prepared for tanning purposes is worth in California $150 per ton, the Commission recommend that the Government have some prepared for shipment to ascertain its quality and value. California now receives its supplies from distant Sicily, while probably the forests of Hamakua and Hilo could supply the whole of the demand of the northwest coast of America. Doubtless many other profitable productions would be thought of if an intelligent and industrious population enjoyed the advantages of these districts. The position which these islands occupy to the west coast of America as its main source of supply in the future of sugar, rice, coffee, &c., guarantee a permanency of values, which should give capital every inducement for investment, and should induce the Government to enter boldly and unhesitatingly into measures to develop these resources, and trust confidently to the increasing value of property to meet the expenses of such improvements. The Districts of Hilo and Hamakua should support a population of 30,000 to 40,000, and the Commission are of opinion that the expense of introducing immigrants and inducing the settlement of these districts by the improvements suggested, will be fully returned to the Government in the increasing revenues of the districts.

Good roads and bridges should be liberally supplied to the Hilo District. The roads at present are not well cared for.

DISTRICT OF PUNA.

This district is largely composed of *a-a* and lava, and no large agricultural enterprises, except stock raising, are being prosecuted at present. The natives of the district, however, look cleanly and contented, and raise some coffee, cocoanuts, &c. The cocoanut grows spontaneously, and its cultivation might be indefinitely extended till the export of copra would be quite important. There is a boat-landing at Mawae, Kula, near Eldart's ranch, to which the present entrance is dangerous in consequence of having to double round a reef of rocks, a part of which might be blasted out, opening a direct channel to a good boat harbor; the expense of which would probably be less than $250. The anchorage is said to be good, and with a good mooring and buoy would supply the district with a fair landing. The roads leading to the harbor would need improvement. The roads generally in the district are good.

DISTRICT OF KAU.

From the crater of Kilauea to Kapapala the country is mostly a grazing country, and is largely owned and leased by the Hawaiian Agricultural Company, who also own between there and Punaluu extensive tracts of sugar lands. There are lands also owned by natives and others in the neighborhood, which are very rich and promise large crops when they shall be cultivated. A good Government road should be opened to the Punaluu landing. The Commission are informed that it is the intention of the Company to erect a large mill on the central factory system, and it will doubtless prove profitable to planters and mill owners. A liberal policy pursued by the Company will doubtless plant a prosperous community there, and open a field for the employment of immigrants. The interests of the Company will compel it to take measures to preserve the forests, in which the Government should co-operate.

The lack of a laboring population will retard the development of this district, which has greater natural advantages than many others. At Honuapo a landing could probably be made by blasting a channel. This land is doubtless well adapted for cultivation. Along the road, mauka, lie the fields of the Naalehu and Waiohinu plantations, running up to an elevation of some 1600 feet. Back of these lands lies a large tract running to an elevation of some 2200 feet, of very rich soil over 5000 acres in extent, abundantly supplied with water for mechanical purposes. At a meeting of the people of Waiohinu complaint was made of the pollution of the water supply, and in view of the necessity of pure water and of preserving and preventing waste of the water which will be necessary hereafter to supply mills, the Commission would recommend that the water course be fenced, and that at some point some 200 feet above the town a reservoir be built with pipes from which householders could be supplied as at Honolulu.

The landing at Kaalualu is good, and should be supplied with a good mooring and buoy. Between Waiohinu and Kahuku are some lands adapted for cane, and might be brought under cultivation if supplied with water for mill purposes. Some 1000 or more acres might here be cultivated. Kahuku, with its neat appointments, shows how pleasant ranch life can be made.

The road to Kona reflects credit on the road supervisor of the district, and should be continued through the Kona district. Over beds of a-a and pahoehoe a fine road is constructed; soil is carried on in some parts and manienie grass planted with the best results. Good roads are a great inducement to settlers, and road supervisors should be held to a strict account. For miles the country seems adapted only to awa, and in some places coffee, and below the forest to goat raising, till the coffee district of Kona is reached. Mr. Greenwell accompanied the Commission to lands on the mountains slopes above Kaawaloa, where at an elevation of 1600 feet a gentle slope upward to an extent of 3000 acres is doubtless well adapted to coffee. It is to be hoped that the capacity of this land will soon be demonstrated, and that the proprietor will succeed in inducing settlers to occupy it. The soil and climate of Kona are adapted to orange and coffee culture, and if the blight can be overcome it will be a prosperous district.

The wharf at Kaawaloa, which has been allowed to fall into ruin, should be repaired. The roads in the Kona district are very discreditable, and should be put in order as soon as possible.

As roads are so important in the development of the resources of every district, your Commission would call the attention of the

Government to the bad results of the present system of working out the road tax. Road Supervisors find that they cannot get fair work out of the people, and we would therefore recommend that the taxes be collected in money, and be used in employing the labor of competent men under the direction of skilful road makers.

The Commission would recommend that all buoys laid out at the different landings in the Kingdom should be carefully laid, and that in all cases the length of cable should be equal to three times the depth of the water; and every three months the buoys should be examined and painted, and the cable hove up to ascertain if it is foul. They recommend spar buoys where the depth of water is not over eight fathoms, and iron nun buoys in deeper water. Much could be saved by care.

Your Commissioners have not attempted to make estimates of the quantities of arable lands in the districts, as in the absence of accurate surveys such estimates must be based entirely upon conjecture, as also estimates of the cost of the improvements suggested, which we recommend should be estimated by the Superintendant of Public Works, or other practical authority.

(The Commission embarked at Kailua on the 20th of March, on board H. B. M. Ship "Fantome," Captain Maquay, for Maui,) and beg to express their sense of obligation to H. B. M. Commissioner and Consul General, to Captains Long and Maquay and the officers of the "Fantome," for their many attentions.

HENRY A. P. CARTER,

JNO. M. KAPENA,

JAMES MAKEE.

www.ingramcontent.com/pod-product-compliance
Lightning Source LLC
LaVergne TN
LVHW010832120826
845149LV00016B/1323
* 9 7 8 1 4 1 8 1 8 9 7 2 3 *